EASY A'S

WORK SMARTER, NOT HARDER

KANISHA ARORA

Contents

Preface

Welcome. I am glad you're here. And I want you to know that you matter and that whatever you're facing is valid.

The academic system can be tough plenty. No wonder we have witnessed so many suicides owing to the pressures arising out of it. You may be juggling god knows what problems with your exams and in such situations, how can your school be your priority?

The academic system wouldn't consider your 'out of class' life, but this book does. I want you to feel that this is just another one of your friends, maybe an older sister writing to you recommending some techniques to smash those exams. Let this be your safe space.

For the next few weeks (or however long it takes for you to complete this book), let this be your haven and I can promise you that you'll find something new as you read by. I have tried to make this book fun and an easy read. So that anyone across high school, or even younger than that can easily understand the basics of it. That is also why I've kept it small and handy.

Easy A. Let us break that down. The best grade can be achieved easily with the right techniques and methods. Study smart, not hard.

This book is a compilation of all the techniques I've personally tried and tested over the past years and I've done the necessary research for you.

My name is Kanisha Arora and I'm a 16-year-old CBSE student. I have achieved all A's or A* in my previous grade (11) and current ongoing 12th. What makes me the ideal person to write this book? I wasn't an overachiever back in middle or or even till sophomore year but I transformed with the help of these techniques and methods. And hopefully, you can too. As someone who has been through what you're going through right now, whether it is a slump or some grey cloud you're facing outside school, I can help you. At least in the academic sector anyways. This book is multifaceted and it welcomes all parts of you with open hands.

Just promise yourself not to read and nod all knowingly but actually put the methods to practice. Action counts. This is a story of how I transformed. Of productivity and motivation. I am no expert or professional, but I know what worked for me, hopefully, It'll work for you too.

Acknowledgements

First and foremost, the exam system- the one that made me want to write this book in the first place. It was almost therapeutic writing about you and making it through. You make millions of students' life a living hell each day but they come out stronger so accept this token of thanks.

It now feels right to acknowledge the most important people in my life.

Mom. Thank you for loving us every day. You sacrifice so much for us and go days without being acknowledged. Thank you for being my biggest cheerleader, my favourite person and for helping me get through the toughest moments of my life. You've been patient with me and let me spread my wings. Thank you for believing in me. For seeing that fire and letting me go. You're capable of doing so much. You already possess the magic. I love you, forever.

Papa. You're the reason I am able to make it through any of my endeavours and projects. Your unwavering optimism and action-oriented attitude inspire me every day. Thank you for teaching me it's okay not to win sometimes. To live with the knowledge that you didn't make it and still keep going. It's the most important lesson. Thank you for bringing home 1 book home each day so we could have a plethora of self-help books to read and evolve from. It'll be very difficult to fill your shoes and live up to you. But If I achieve even half of what you have today, I'll consider myself successful. I love you and I cherish you every day.

To M, You make every day fun. I enjoy having sleepless nights full of philosophies and our favourite karaoke. Our band remains incomplete. If we would have explored music further, I'm sure we'd be the endgame brother-sister duo today. Not that we aren't right now. I cherish our secret lists, unspoken reading sessions, guess in 10 games, blue (remember?) and most of all you. And I don't hate you. Not even a little bit. Not even at all. (that's all the love you're getting from me today).

To my grandparents, who I can always count on no matter what. I'm sorry I don't spend enough time with you. I know you always want what is in my best interests and I'm grateful.

Dadi, a special note for you – you're my favourite *choti* dadi, I loved our movie marathons and *tombola* sessions. I remember braiding your hair as a kid. I'd like to do that again. I PROMISE I'll spend more time with you now. After all, you are my best friend.

To Aishi, my chosen family. You make the distinction between friends and family. To our unending rants , spicy gossiping, crying sessions, weekly checkups, the best-ever code names and my personal favourite boy talks. You make 4648 miles seem close. I cannot wait to hug you the next time I see you. Love you, endlessly.

To my senior teachers, who went above and beyond for me. You are immaculate. I'm here because of you. Thank you for always motivating me.

To my friends, you know you're cherished. You make my days less shitty. Thank you for putting up with me every day. I love you plenty.

And to the world unknown. My future. Everything I do is dedicated to you. I can't wait to see what's out there for me. Thank you for being my source of motivation. I hope I'll make you proud.

CHAPTER ONE

Motivation

The basis of it all. Motivation is key to achieving anything you want in your life. Do you want to achieve something? Learn how to light that fire. It is not like you wake up one day and decide that u want to achieve that A grade. It takes practice. It is an essential factor that changes positive thought into instant action. It switches a great idea into action and can undoubtedly affect the world around you.

Motivation is a force to push you closer toward your dream. If Steve Jobs lacked the motivation to launch Apple, you would not get an iPhone or iPad. It gives one a purpose to live with a forever smile on the face. Thus, realizing and working on your self-motivation skills will make you capable of taking control of different aspects of life including your academics.

The critical elements of self-motivation are resilience and optimism. The former will help you bounce back during difficult times, whereas later, you will show you a brighter side ahead. This way, you will be able to control the emotions that are holding you back.

Whether personal or professional events both demand a person to stay positive to achieve the goals. As a motivated person, you will always try to push your limits and develop your performance level every day. And that is the reason that it is the most important step in your journey to advance your grades.

As per psychology, motivation comes from intrinsic or extrinsic sources.

Intrinsic Motivation - Intrinsic comes from a love of learning and the process itself. Taking studying for instance. It's about taking joy in studying and dwelling happily in the process of it. It's about being eager to learn new things and being fascinated by the new information. It's looking forward to answering that test you studied so well for. It isn't about the final reward or destination, but about the journey of it all. For instance, I am very fascinated by the laws of human psychology. I remember studying eagerly about it and then applying that new information to my life. I enjoyed the feeling of knowing something significant that I could use for application. That covers intrinsic motivation.

Extrinsic Motivation - Whereas sometimes, it is the extrinsic sources of motivation pushing us towards excellence. It includes the positive reinforcements, the end result, and the rewards bestowed upon us when we achieve that goal of ours. One doesn't necessarily need to enjoy or care about the process as long as they are getting the desired end results. This kind of motivation pulls us along in short term. It is guided by outcomes. I myself remember wanting to pull up my game in sophomore examinations in order to gain verbal appraise from my parents. A sense of appreciation. That was my motivation then.

So it doesn't matter which kind of source you have for your motivation, as long as it works for you. You could have intrinsic, extrinsic, or possibly both. Most people have a mixture of the two. It is all about understanding what efforts you have to put in now to create your image of the

Future You.

<u>Start With 'Why'</u>

Puja Puneet, a renowned speaker from *club success Gyan,* once revealed in her podcast that when you're setting a goal, it isn't about the what or the how, it's about the *why.* Not about what grade you want or how you will achieve it but *why* you want to attain it. Ask yourself why your goal is important to you. Why are you so set to work for it? What is it going to change for you?

Is it because you enjoy the process of learning but the pursuit of better grades seems even more important? Or maybe you want to catch up to peer pressure and prove yourself to people? Or you're working your way into your dream college?

Whatever it is, you need to figure your *why* out and it needs to be long-term. Knowing your *why* is going to keep you going for a longer period of time to maintain your sense of motivation till you achieve your goal. Channel your *why* when your temporary feeling of passion or fire fades.

The 3 challenges stopping our growth-

It can be hard to stay motivated when you feel like it is you against the world. The cause of lack of intrinsic motivation can be laid down into 3 factors- laziness, conformity and circumstances.

1. **Laziness-** We are in an era. An era of digitalisation with complete comfort. Then GEN Z believes in means of instant gratification and hence working hard to get that bread doesn't seem interesting. In an age where we get entertained by scrolling our fingers through countless reels, everything manages to grab our attention for only a span of seconds. This is the age of distraction. We've been trained to tailor our lives to what we find immediately interesting. If we don't like something we swipe. But when this

translates to our academics, things don't remain comfortable anymore. It is unfortunate that we cannot study the subjects that we are interested in only. We have to take in the whole package. We don't absorb new concepts in six seconds and it isn't interesting anymore. We cant scroll when the text gets boring.

It is this, a compilation of shorter attention spans, the need to stay entertained 24/7 and thousands of sources of distraction that make us lazy. Why learn political science question answers when I can just as easily watch *the vampire diaries* on Netflix?

We need to focus on this lack of inspiration that is pulling us back. It is time to light that fire again. You need to start finding reasons that make your most difficult or hated subject interesting. How that political science chapter is actually an enigma of how your country runs. How conflicts don't just exist in the lives of laymen but also in the context of big, superpowers. Learn to broaden your perspective about the world. This makes u equipped with a proactive approach.

At our academic premises, we r never encouraged to look beyond our books- novels, books, youtube videos, documentaries etc. If u hate a subject, dare to ask yourself why. Is it hard or have u just not tried it with an open mind yet? Are u blinded by the common perceptions? Do u hate it because ur friends do so? Become self-aware and inspire yourself. Smash procrastination by learning to love those subjects. If anyone can do it it's you. Know that deep inside and you'll achieve what you want. Have faith in yourself. Enough faith to keep you going. Enough faith to keep you motivated. Dive deep into the subject you're pursuing and give it your all. Learn to love its best parts and ignore the others. That's how champions win and that's how you can win too. As they say, it's all in the head. Decide today. Take the oath today that you won't be lazy anymore and stick to it like it's a matter of life and death. Like it's your last day on earth and this is the one thing that matters most. Like you cannot go one day without working in its absence.

There are mental resistances which form as aspects of laziness. The barriers that stop you from your own progress. By taking action. The infamous little voice in the head that keeps telling you that you can play video games a few more hours, watch a couple more episodes and read just a handful more pages of your favourite fantasy- is the one that you need to be aware of more. Stop self-sabotaging and take control of your life.

2. Conformity – If I had a nickel for all the times I've downplayed my studies to fit in with my friends and seem cool, id be a billionaire today. We have all done this at least once or twice in our school life. Confirming peer influence and giving in to whatever 'trend' is going on.

We as humans want to seem likeable. We crave the feeling of importance and compliments from people whom we care about. We constantly change our behaviours to fit the definition of cool. Science says that we are a mixture of the 5 closest people to us in our lives. We subconsciously copy them and never realise it. If your friend group doesn't care about school..you'll find that you won't either. If your pals adopt a new trend...SURPRISE- you'll be inclined towards it too.

We do this for social gain. No one wants to be at the rear end of the social ladder and we constantly climb it whether we realise it or not. Feelings of being left out and envy are determining factors for this. Sometimes people gain the titles of 'wannabe' or 'people pleaser' in their attempt at this. This can be detrimental if we look at it from a career point of view. When adapting to the demands of society when you want to seem cool, can conflict with your personal goals. Resulting in decreased self-growth.

Our priorities change and we start focusing on mindless, temporary things instead. Some kids give into substances and that sets their path down to failure if continued relentlessly for a long while. It is necessary to practice moderation or life will eat you up. You'll lose the sense of your future and set yourself up for ruin.

It is important to recognise this at an early stage. If your peer group is interfering with your work and school, you have some serious thinking to do. Don't let your priorities change. Read some self-help books if necessary to gain your self-confidence back. Work on yourself. Make a routine. Do everything in your power to get yourself back and it is guaranteed that with consistent efforts you'll be back on track. Instilling some self-discipline can help too. People say that exercise brings a lot of motivation and discipline to humans. You can try that. Or whatever it is that appeals most to you. Whichever recreational activity stands out best to you. Choose it and let it transform you into a self-disciplined individual.

Except this make sure you surround yourself with people who encourage you to achieve your best not the ones who bring you down. Make sure your best friends are your biggest cheerleaders and not judgmental falsies. Your group, your tribe as they say – describes your vibe. Don't pollute it, it is your most important asset.

Be mentally strong. Gain resilience and learn to give a blind ear to all those who sideline you from your path. It is all that matters. Just have a laser focus, a determined mindset and strong willpower. These are the qualities of the world's most successful people and surely they will help you out too. It is of extreme importance to keep your values in mind while ascertaining certain commitments. Know what interferes with your future and scrap it out of your life. If you are able to figure out your barriers then- firstly you're a legend for being to deep-sighted and having enough self-awareness to rise above your shortcomings. secondly identify ways to effectively counter it with a conscious mind.

Rest assured, if you practice the given strategies for this one, you are good to go.

3. Circumstances- Everyonehas something or the other occupying their lives except academics. Some people don't have access to enough resources. Some, have deteriorating family issues, and Some are juggling with diseases. Some have toxicity in the form of fake friends surrounding them. The list goes on and so do the problems. But the academic system isn't fair. It doesn't take into account what your 'situation' is when assigning you a grade. It only measures your value in terms of the marks you got in your finals/ midterms and that is supposed to define you as a human being.

Well, I accept that it is wrong. It isn't appropriate to judge a person by their ratification

skills, ignoring all other aspects of them that make them who they are. You exist outside of your academic premises and I acknowledge that. But I cannot let you excuse your studies in exchange for presenting how unbearable your situation is. You got problems, I get it. But you cannot run away from what matters for your future at the moment; exams.

Use your inner fire to light passion in you. Let this be your perennial source of motivation. Did you face issues at home? Challenge yourself! Test yourself by seeing if you can handle both. If you can ace your academics with that much going on in your mind. Imagine what else you can do. It really does make you a legend. Glorify your achievements when you have any. Let yourself know that it's okay to celebrate too. You have worked hard and you deserve to be celebrated. Treat yourself to ice cream or gelato or whatever it is that makes you happy. This will be your reinforcement and it'll make you want to achieve more. A classical example of classic & operant conditioning.

Don't let your grades define you but don't let your circumstances do that either. Broaden the definition of yourself. Make use of what you have. Be grateful for each and everything that helps you get through your day. Show compassion to the objects/people that make you smile every day. It starts with your mindset. If you believe that you can overcome whatever is holding you back then you can. However, if you don't trust your strength, then I'm sorry no one, and I mean no one can make you shift that. You are your only barrier and you are bigger and stronger than what you're going through. Practice these affirmations every single day and you'll already be surrounded by a positive vibe and aura. Only the moving past will be left. Know that you can handle it. Have enough faith in yourself as I do in you. The fact that you have made it this far ahead in the book bears testimony to the fact that you care. You care about your future, and your academics and you're willing to change. Accepting the problem is the first and most difficult step in overcoming it. And I hold you in my highest regard for that.

To round the chapter up Motivation is not some gift from the heavens above that is blessed upon to only god's favourites. It is recognising that you want something,why you want it bad enough and then let the feeling stay.

CHAPTER TWO

Growth Mindset

The concept of a growth mindset – the belief that intelligence can be developed through effort – is gaining considerable attention in the education world. And for good reason. One of the most important factors that help individuals succeed in life, is their growth mindset. It says that *you* yourself define your work ethic. Change your words, change your mindset.

What is a Fixed Mindset vs. a Growth Mindset?

The theory of a fixed and growth mindset comes from Dr Carol Dweck, a professor of psychology at Stanford University.

- **Fixed Mindset** – Students with a fixed mindset believe their skills, talents and overall intelligence are fixed traits. They may believe that any challenges they face are because they lack natural skills and talent. Or they may think they "aren't good enough", so they refuse to try an assignment that seems too hard. In the classroom setting, believing you are "good at writing" or "bad at writing" is an example of a fixed mindset.

- <u>**Growth Mindset**</u> – Students with a growth mindset believe they can develop their skills and talents through effort, persistence and practice. They generally believe they are capable of learning nearly anything if they have the right focus, and they typically have the motivation to persevere after mistakes. Because they believe they can improve through hard work and trying new learning methods, they are more receptive to lessons and feedback.

Individuals who believe their talents can be developed (through hard work, good strategies, and input from others) have a <u>growth mindset</u>. They tend to achieve more than those with a more fixed mindset (those who believe their talents are innate gifts). This is because they worry less about looking smart and they put more energy into learning. Anyone who is willing to improve themselves and is willing to have a learner's attitude automatically has a growth mindset regardless of their source of motivation.

Now the term 'growth mindset' has become a buzzword in this generation, used loosely here and there. But upon looking, I wonder if people's idea of this term is limited. Upon researching, I have come across the following misconceptions, that people may have-

1) I already have it, and I always have. People often confuse a growth mindset with being flexible or open-minded or with having a positive outlook — qualities they believe they've simply always had. My colleagues and I call this a false growth mindset. Everyone is actually a mixture of fixed and growth mindsets, and that mixture continually evolves with experience. A "pure" growth mindset doesn't exist, which we have to acknowledge in order to attain the benefits we seek.

2) A growth mindset is just about praising and rewarding effort. This isn't true for students in schools, and it's not true for employees in organizations. In both settings, outcomes matter. An unproductive effort is never a good thing. It's critical to reward not just effort but learning and progress and to emphasize the processes that yield these things, such as seeking help from others, trying new strategies, and capitalizing on setbacks to move forward effectively. In all of our research, the outcome — the bottom line — follows from deeply engaging in these processes.

3) Just espouse a growth mindset, and good things will happen. Mission statements are wonderful things. You can't argue with lofty values like growth, empowerment, or innovation. But what do they mean to employees if the company doesn't implement policies that make them real and attainable? They just amount to lip service. Organizations that embody a growth mindset encourage appropriate risk-taking, knowing that some risks won't work out. They reward employees for important and useful lessons learned, even if a project does not meet its original goals. They support collaboration across organizational boundaries rather than competition among employees or units. They are committed to the growth of every member, not just in words but in deeds, such as broadly available development and advancement opportunities. And they continually reinforce growth mindset values with concrete policies.

Tips on How to Develop a Growth Mindset
Embrace your imperfections-No one has learned anything valuable without making mistakes. Changing your

perspective on mistakes is one of the greatest gifts you can give yourself. View yourmistakes as one of the many steps toward mastery. Take time t reflect on both successes and failures. Remember that everyone succeeds and fails, and that each step we took got us to where we are today.

<u>See challenges as opportunities for growth</u>-Once you embrace your imperfections, you can view your mistakes as helpful. The red pen isn't the enemy—not trying is. One practical way to encourage your attitude is to take the most common mistakes that the you made on a test or quiz and analyse those mistakes. The more open everyone is about the mistakes they've made, the less significance theyplace on future errors.

<u>Adopt a "growth mindset" language</u> -Another valuable strategy is to replace negative words with positive phrases. For example, use the term "learning" instead of "failing." And use the phrase "not yet." Whenever you struggle with a task, just know that you haven't mastered it yet. Pay attention to words that may reinforce one mindset or the other. Some phrases that support a fixed mindset include: "I'm so smart"; "Wrong answer"; and "I'm a natural at this." On the other hand, some words and phrases that support a growth mindset include: "Mistakes help me learn"; "Great use of several strategies to solve that problem"; and "I haven't been able to solve this problem yet, but I will."

<u>Acknowledge your efforts</u>-When fostering a growth mindset in yourself, remember to acknowledge the process and effort you're making, rather than the outcome alone. Praise yourself for practising, asking for help or trying new strategies, rather than on your talent or intellect. Reward yourself for how hard you've worked or how much you are progressing. Remember that hard work always comes before obtaining skill—and that learning is a process.

FEAR OF FAILURE-
"am I hard on me?"
I ask myself.
"Sure, it's what keeps me going."
I believe it was grade 11 mid-term when I realised my potential again and marks started meaning more than just marks to me. It was a bittersweet epiphany. I scored well now. I was glad. In the beginning, I just studies to test my potential in my choice of subjects. With time it developed into a feeling of high. Yeah is it believable? Grades can give you a high too. And a level so high that you can't help but yearn for more of it. Obsess it. Put all your time and energy into it.

With this amount of dedication, imagine if the marks don't turn out satisfiable. It will crush your world. That's what it did to me. After preparing from 7 help books, putting in a 100 hour of work to each subject, sacrificing parties and get-togethers to 'study', when the required grade isn't obtained, it breaks you from within and you start asking these strange questions to yourself-

"Was it all for nothing Kanisha?"

"All that time spent, energy lost and instilling faux hope? Did it really go waste?"

"Am i the problem here, is my best effort not good enough?"

"Where could I have gone wrong?"

Caught in this labyrinth of endless questions and seemingly no answer to be found. It puts you in a quake, difficult to get out of. This cycle persists in every household. Between peer reputation, teachers you don't want to let down, parents who you want to please and most of all our own highly exceeded expectations from ourselves put this heavy burden on us which is impossible to be met every time. This inevitably breeds fear of failure. You come in a 'do or die situation' and when your efforts don't prove to be enough, you get caved. It's natural. To work so hard for something for such a long time only to fail? I ask you- Who wouldn't give up in such a situation? That's what it is. Giving up. It can be tempting but it'll defy the whole purpose of this process. That is to fulfil your potential. To self-actualise to the fullest. Apply Alfred Adler's individual psychology and instead of giving in to your defeats, learn to set a fire in yourself ignited by them. Use it to your advantage and bounce back stronger than ever.

For so long I decided my value on my grades. I tested my worth each and every time I got my result and that is probably the reason why I shed tears when even a single mark was lost. When others were celebrating passing the examination, I was in a dilemma wondering if I should give up. If I should let the 5 marker question where I lost marks, get to me. The automated answer was always yes.

It was a while before I rectified this mindset of mine. I'm not going to blabber about how grades are an indicator of our progress. No, because that was what it was for me and I still managed to hurt myself along the way. No, but they definitely are reality checks. A tough

knock on the door, bump on the head and clap in the face. You need to work harder. Apparently, your preparation lacked and it's better you realise it and learn to accept it sooner than later.

A failure is a tool for growth. Learning from mistakes is a product of failure.

That's all it is. A chance to learn. A chance to reflect. A chance to improve. A chance to work on your shortcomings. For a better result next time. It isn't a definite judgement of your capabilities. But it is a gift. A gift meant to help you be in touch with reality so that when it's time for you to perform on the biggest platform, you're prepared. You're prepared with all your gut and you're ready to kill it there.

Take the positive aspect. Apply the proactive approach here. It will be difficult. No denying that. When are shoulders are burdened by the weight of expectations from those who surround us, we are at a loss. It gets difficult to look at failure in any respect except negative. When your own expectations are not giving you space to breathe, imagine the burden from everyone else's. That nemesis in class who would love nothing more than to see that B on your answer sheet. Your teachers expect the most out of you in class and constantly measure your potential based on your marks. Your parents who even though would love you no matter what, but you will only earn their *respect* through your achievements. Your siblings constantly look up to you. In such situations, every grade matters. Every paper matters. Every answer wrong matters. In such a world, there is no room for mistakes. Only excellence can persist. Only A* are acceptable. Anyone who scores anything below that is considered and rendered as a failure. Then start the waterworks. The realisation of having failed in your attempt to excel. The fact that you let down not just everyone else, but yourself too. How would you ever overcome this? Would you ever be able to?

The answer here against all probabilities is yes. Yes, you will overcome it. Only if you allow yourself to. You need to allow room for mistakes. To err is to be human. Cmon you know that. You know better than sulking after a bad grade. No. Take responsibility and accept it. MOVE ON. It's okay. It's okay. You'll be okay. Even if it may feel like the end of the world at the moment.

Cultivating a growth mindset is one of the 7 strategies that will help you advance in your studies.

planning and making to-do lists

Benjamin Franklin once said, "If you fail to plan, you plan to fail." I live by this considering the depth of it. Planning your day out in advance can give you a sense of confidence and purpose. It sets out your day's routine in front of you and ensures that

you rule your day and not the other way around.

Your plan out doesn't have to be that fancy and decorative if you don't want to devote time to such stuff but making it presentable doesn't hurt anyone either.

You do you bestie <3

I was raised by my mom and dad asking me to plan my days on the basis of the grade I want to achieve.

"Kanisha, have you planned your day for tomorrow? Written your course of action eh?"

To which I would roll my eyes, fret over and groan.No one likes to be reminded of their failure to keep up with the only task assigned to them. And I certainly wasn't a fan of confrontation.

I would lie and *then* take out my mini notebook which had a 'game plan written over it in round hand calligraphy. It was my book of plans for world domination, as my dad used to call it. Then I would make my to-do list for the day after.

I have been practising this for the past 5 years of my life, ever since 7th grade and even though I would never accept it in front of my parents, it has added a whole lot of value to my life.

In the following pages, I'll be mentioning a few pros of planning your day out in advance

be it the last thing you do before sleeping or the first thing you do when you wake up.

I'm going to let you decide for yourself.

Pros of making to-do lists

1. Feel Good Factor- Writing things down helps reduce stress and makes you feel more relaxed. This also helps you remember all tasks for the day and ensures that nothing slips out of your mind. You don't have to work around your day carrying the load of a gazillion tasks in your head making sure you don't forget any one and mess up.

Setting a schedule provides composure. It is no surprise that billionaires from around the world use this technique and are infinitely more powerful and confident as a result. You get a feeling of being in control of your life and actions.

Also, the act of crossing tasks down at the end of completion delivers a sense of accomplishment and motivates you to keep walking this path. It serves as a reward for a task well done.

2. It will help you achieve goals- It's tough to achieve big goals when they seem to overwhelm you. As a consequence, it's easy to procrastinate on them. One of the best ways to solve this problem is by breaking down a large goal into smaller parts. This is where a to-do list becomes significant. It lets you make large and overwhelming projects manageable.

Also, you get more done by focusing on high-value activities. Once you have a list of things you need to do, it's much easier to prioritize the tasks on it. This will ensure you're always working on the right things. Otherwise, it's easy to fall into a circle of doing what seems easiest or most urgent. Doing this may result in skipping important things that don't require your immediate attention.

Another great way to use your to-do list is for analyzing your behaviour later. You can see which activities produced the best results and double down on them. This makes it easy to identify opportunities to focus on and things to drop off your schedule.

To-do lists also help you uncover what you don't see at first glance. When you write things down, it forces your brain to think in depth about the task at hand. You may see things that you missed at first, growing your capacity to achieve good results.

Also, mentally manipulating a task makes it much more likely to achieve. The more you think about it, the more it becomes prominent and important to-do in your mind.

Staying focused is difficult with the number ofdistractions in the modern workplace. Therefore, it's easy to get off track but a to-do list can help you get back on it. Seeing a clear outline of what you should be doing can make a huge difference to your productivity.

Last but not least, creating a to-do list is in its core a planning process. Planning, in turn, allows for turning abstract goals into concrete steps of action. You remove anxiety by breaking down goals and know what you should be doing at any given time. It's a fine way to maximize your potential to achieve big goals.

3. It is time efficient- You end up saving a lot of time by making a schedule. Devoting just 5 minutes per day to plan it out ultimately turns out to be an investment. Those 5 minutes can save you 2 hours of execution.

It's like making a painting. You don't just dive right in with your colours, but you make a layout with a pencil. A rough sketch to start with, erase the shortcomings on the way and then bring the blueprint to life by painting along the lines.

This is how perfection is created and it is no different from setting plans and goals. The magic happens when you bring your visions, and your written goals to reality by simply following the layout. Whether you're a long-time planner or a night-before crammer, knowing how to timetable your life is an essential skill for when you need to power through your work.

It'll help you be more reliable- Making plans each and every day and ticking them off would give you the confidence to keep going. After a while of doing just this, you would have confidence in your activity and in yourself to complete the tasks you assign yourself.

Hence, comes reliability. Your ability to complete self-instructed tasks will enhance thereby increasing your productivity ten folds. Now, who wouldn't want that?

Now that we have discussed *why* you need to make to-do lists, it's time to tackle the *how*.

To crack the code to this you need to ask yourself certain questions.

1. What holds priority for you- what is the most unfamiliar topic/subject? What demands urgency?

2. What is your deadline?- when do your tentative exams begin?

3. What else do you have going on?- what besides your academics, is taking up your time?

Let us go through each of these questions one by one and tackle this.

1. Prioritise- At the moment, all your topics and subjects that need to be ticked off are in a scattered web of unorganised clatter. You need to detangle each thought and organise it in the order of its importance.

Is there a particular subject where you lack? Is there a reason why you excel in psychology but fail tragically in economics? Are you finding the demand-supply curve of economics difficult? Are phenomena of areal differentiation eating you up? Is there a particular subject where you want to score more this time? Have you studied political science in the past 1 month? Do you tend to spend all your time studying English and sideline other subjects, picking favourites? Are you biased in your studying approach? Are you willing to prioritise???

If you can sing Taylor swift's *love story* without blinking once or rap that drake's song without letting out a singer shudder, why can't you know your subjects this well as well? RANK YOUR SUBJECTS AND TOPICS. Do this as a first step rest will take place smoothly. Be honest with yourself and don't skip this phase.

2. Draft a Timetable- Yes it's important and no you don't get to skip this. It is of paramount importance that you understand the urgency of your deadline and the work that needs to be done in time. I don't need to elaborate on the repercussions if you procrastinate this and put it off for the next day until its finally your exam day and you're dying under the excruciating stress.

There is a range of apps that you can download to help you facilitate this process. Calendar functions on the *notion*, *notes*, *my study life* and google docs. Of course, we wouldn't forget to include the classic pen and paper along with a complimentary bullet journal.

Make it look attractive and decorative so that you're inclined to complete it sooner and tick off those boxes in your bullet journal. Use highlighters, colour pens and stickers of your choice to enhance the appeal.

This is done to ensure your attention towards the plan and maintain consistency in your urge to follow it. Look at it like this – the better it looks, the more you'll want to look at it. The more you look at it, the more you'll be reminded of your tasks of the day.

There come some specialised journals for the same. *To do tick journals, YOUR DAILY PLAN* and *daily planners* of different sorts. You may choose your pick and decide what best suits you. Consider this step an important one as the journal you pick today, will be with you for the rest of the year. It will define your aura and will be a testimony to your experiences. So pay attention to selection.

Experiment, try out new things. Decide what works for you and take your time. But most importantly, ***START.***

Take the first step of many, to the life unlived.

alter the course of your life, step outside your boundaries and do what was till now rendered unthinkable. Don't derail your own progress by coming to your biggest source of resistance. That is the most important thing. Be mindful of it.

The extent to detailing in your timetable is your discretion. You can go all in and mention time to time slots will each slot allotted to a particular activity or task, or you could just mention the tasks you're supposed to complete on the day and move forward with it without compromising any time.

3. Other activities- I don't expect you to devote 100% of your time to your academics. Everyone has hobbies, extracurricular activities and in most cases when it comes to high school seniors- profile enhancements to focus on. They may seem even more important at some point in time in comparison to academics and therefore I urge you to take time out for them guilt-free. Take time out for all your necessities. Be it self-care or sports. Ask yourself questions like – Are you spending enough time relaxing? Is your sleep schedule up to the mark?

Execution

A perfect plan would remain useless until and unless it is implemented at the right juncture. I have seen countless people who formulate great plans and have a boundless imagination but fail to put those ideas to work. In my opinion, any lamen can dream and think of ideas, but only people with great willpower and clarity will actually work towards it. Implementation is just like making a timetable or to-do list if not more.

the execution of a perfect plan is the next level of progress as a morale booster that can turn a dream into reality through practical application. It is the second step after planning. Many times we as students lack implementation. Procrastination is one reason why.

Procrastination

Have you ever put off your homework till the last minute? Or perhaps studied for the test only a day before? Maybe delayed writing an essay till the last possible hour? All of us are guilty of delaying tasks and putting off important work until a later date. This is essentially procrastinating. It is the action of purposefully delaying any task or activity. So we ask ourselves this question – why do people procrastinate even when they are so busy most of the time? We live in the 21st century, where time is our most precious commodity. And yet, we waste this precious resource procrastinating our time away.

The reasons for a person procrastinating can be varied. It depends on person-to-person and situation-to-situation. However, there are some universal reasons that cause people to delay their tasks and actions.

1. Procrastination due to fear of failure

One of the most important ones is the fear of failure. When a person delays doing an important task or is disinterested in finishing it, the cause could be a deep-rooted fear of failure. It is in human nature to avoid and fear failure. When we dedicate ourselves to something and put our heart and soul into it, we naturally expect positive results. When we don't get positive results it breaks our spirit and sense of motivation. Therefore, as a defence mechanism, we choose not to finish the task so that we can avoid the consequences as well.

2. Lack of Clarity

Another reason is the lack of focus and determination. Feeling directionless and unfocused can often cause people to lose interest in their studies and the constant need to give up altogether would linger on. This leads to procrastination. Sometimes the lack of goals and objectives is also the reason a person loses their focus. Since they do not have an end goal in mind, they end up wasting energy on other useless tasks. For example- if a student has no motivation to succeed in their academics, he/she wouldn't have a *why* in mind to study.

3. Perfectionism

There are other reasons a person may procrastinate. Sometimes, a person may be too much of a perfectionist. This distracts them from other tasks. And then there are other reasons like laziness, low energy levels, easy distractions, etc.

Example- I have a friend who is a perfectionist and she wants everything on fleek. As a people pleaser, she can't help to escape this quality of hers. Because of this, she devotes too much time to one project and ends up procrastinating others. As a consequence, most of her tasks derail.

WAYS TO COUNTER PROCRASTINATION

One way to stop procrastinating is to break down the dreaded task into little steps. If the work or the task is too overwhelming, we tend to procrastinate about it. But if the job is broken down, then we can tackle one step at a time without being overwhelmed. You can also create a detailed timetable or a timeline of some sort to help you with the steps.

At other times changing your work environment may be beneficial. It can provide you with the boost necessary to stop procrastinating and finish the task. If possible get a friend or a parent to keep a check on your progress. It helps keep the motivation levels up and encourages you to finish the task on time.

The main concern is not to over-focus or blame yourself for procrastinating sometimes. We are all a victim of procrastination from time to time. As long as it does not derail your entire schedule, give yourself a break and just get back to your studies.

Productivity Hacks

Can you define productivity for me? Is it devoting 12 living hours of daylight towards studying and studying only? Living on the brink of insanity? Working in offices 7 days of the week to come up with the same 5 principles each day? productivity is whatever you choose, define it but in formalised terms, it means spending your time well. It needs to add value to your life by getting work done efficiently. It is about optimising your day, and your hours to do everything that will contribute to the future *you*. It means getting enough work done so you can now take time out for your leisure activities, guilt-free. To me, that is productivity. Doing what needs to be done. Following a certain schedule and emerging victoriously. Time well spent.

Now let us talk about specific strategies laid down to make big, complex tasks seem easy and basic. Know that 11 hours of productive work done is always better than a whole day of just staring at the text whose intimidation keeps increasing by the hour.

1. Pomodoro Technique- At this point in time I am sure you must have heard of this technique since it's basically all over youtube. But even if you aren't, I'll be providing a gist of it.

I wholeheartedly introduce you to the best productivity hack in the history of hacks- The Pomodoro technique. I first got to know about it in one of these *study smart* youtube videos when I was cramming for 10th-grade board exams. It has revolutionised my studying ever since. It basically uses a timer to divide your whole work into meaningful chunks (25), separated by short breaks. It was developed by an Italian named Francesco Cirillo in the late 1980s. It laid the foundation that the human brain has an attention span. It can't focus on a designated task with full capacity post that span. Its working is as follows-

1. choose a task. Eg- complete the french revolution unit.

2. Set a 25-minute timer.

3. spend those 25 minutes focusing exclusively on the assigned task. The catch here is – if you get distracted or start procrastinating. You have to start the timer again.

4. Post your time completion, and give yourself a 5-minute break.

5. Choose another task and the cycle goes on.

Each 'Pomodoro' allows you to get in the zone. Your most attentive state of mind and apply all your concentration to one and on the task only. Instead of wasting days and days finding the perfect study technique, use this. Because your time is precious, devoting all your time in the name of *hack hunting*

defies the whole process of study hacks. There are specific websites that might aid you in this expedition. They already have timers set for 25 minutes and you just have to press start.

The most difficult step of all in this is starting. Taking the first step. We usually verify the process of studying to such degraded levels that when one actually sits to study they realise the fear was all made up. It's actually a lot easier to just give in and face your responsibilities. Hence the greatest fear, as they say, is fear itself. Odds are, the hardest part was just starting.

2. Journaling- Encourage your productivity by following the given steps.

- **Brain Dumping**- we often get burdened with the number of things, and tasks we are supposed to do and it starts affecting us mentally if we don't do anything about it. Enter- brain dumping. Write down every task that scares you. That has been on your mind. All the scary deadlines, and project submissions, force you to pull all-nighters. These thoughts become heavy until and unless you pen them down somewhere. Brain dumping in its literal sense is dumping your burdens. Making your headlight. It can be described as therapeutic, at least for me. When we have a number of tasks to do then it becomes confusing and we can't sort out their importance so we end up messing up all of them. In reality, each task needs its own attention and brain dumping can help you sort. You don't have to remember your burdens anymore. You have them jotted down. You're free, mentally speaking. Go crazy! Word vomit!

- **Specify, Select and prioritise-** Now that you have your tasks in front of you can sort and get clear about what needs to be done. Write the deadlines in front of the tasks that you have written in order so that you can arrange them chronologically according to your priority. It goes without saying that the tasks that you have a sooner deadline must be completed sooner and the ones that have significant time left to be completed can be put off for a while. This is an important but not the only basis you must use to organise your schedule. The subjects that are difficult to you must be given priority since you know how stressed you get when you have to do those in the end. So save yourself from your own designated hell and get the tougher tasks over with. You know you have to.

- **Practicality-** Make sure that the time slots you assign yourself are practical and can be managed, or you'll begin to lose confidence and motivation running after an unrealistic schedule, humanly impossible to follow.

Know your limits and capabilities and save yourself from burnout. Write down roughly how long each task would take you and then add 10 more minutes to it for emergencies. This way you're being realistic and can relax from time to time.

As we come to the end of this chapter, I implore you to ask yourself some questions that may seem a little difficult to answer but try not to be biased here. Do you take time out to work for your goals? Is it enough? How can you make it enough? How can you use these hacks to double your productivity in the same time span?

If you have a bundle of tasks to complete right now and you're putting it off again, this is your sign to do it. I'm channelling motivation and sending this book to you. Go do that task. Tick that box. Feel that power.

CHAPTER FIVE

Mental Health

I have a secret for you. It might disturb you but it's true and you need to know it.

You're not good enough. But it's okay.

There are numerous times in our lives when we doubt our capabilities. If everything one achieved till now was a fluke, or if they actually deserved it.

Did you get that debate award because the person who was better than you wasn't present? Did you get that A in your exam because the paper was unusually easy? Was the only reason that you got selected for that student council position, that the best-suited person for it didn't apply? Is everything that you have achieved till now actually just handed to you, did you even deserve it in the first place? Are you lying to yourself to make yourself feel better? What if you aren't good enough after all?

We all have that one voice in our heads poking and strangling our inner being. Doubting ourselves over and over and whenever we fail to achieve something that we worked hard for, it opens up like a patched-up wound and starts hurting.

I'll share an experience here, quite personal to me but since this is supposed to be a safe space for all of us here, I would like it if you resonated with me and know that we all go through the same things.

It was my 12th-grade summer after the vacations. I had recently been pumped about the school, having a club of my own, being in a core position in the newsletter and scoring marks I was satisfied with. Then came an opportunity I didn't know I needed. A competition to select the best debater across the grade for this national-level competition.

College Application dates were close and I'd be a fool if I wouldn't recognise the effect this would have on my resume. I instantly signed up. Along with 30 other people. There were supposed to be 4-5 rounds for the selection. I knew I'd make it through most of them because I had the experience. And I did. I made it through 4 of the rounds when it came to the top 3 students. The surroundings were tense. If you had told me 3 years ago that I'd be applying for such a competitive position, I wouldn't have believed you. Let's just say I wasn't exactly a go-getter back then. But here I was. In the shortlisted top 3. It was unreal and felt wonderful. My opponents were equally good if not better and it could be any one of us. As you can see, it meant a lot to me. Winning, meant a lot to me. So I put up a challenge with myself, just like I did always. If I won the position, it means I am all that there is, I can achieve anything and I am capable of whatever I put my mind to. I am good enough. And if I didn't. If I didn't, all this hard work, months of preparation, research, and pining would be for nothing. I would have failed and I would turn out to be average. Average like any other kid in class. But at the time I pushed that thought away and waited patiently for the results.

The day came. I was supposed to anchor an assembly that day. The same assembly in which the results would be announced. Imagine how I must have felt when the vice principal called out a name that wasn't mine for the post. I'll make it easy for you.

I smiled. I smiled because she deserved it. Because she worked equally as hard as I did for it and she would be the ideal candidate. I smiled and I clapped for her. Truly happy for her, I realised. I was, however, holding back tears. Tears for I didn't get selected. Tears for I couldn't win the challenge. Tears for I really wasn't good enough.

I had to go back up on the stage and end the assembly. I did that with the widest smile ever on my face. And when it ended, I ran to the washroom. Ran and cried. Cried for what felt like hours. Because this time, I failed. I failed myself, I failed my parents and I failed my teachers. Everyone kept asking me that day if I was okay. I wasn't. I didn't tell anyone that though.

It's been 3 months since that happened. I convinced myself that maybe I had better things waiting for me and getting that position would have interfered with it. But It still hurts me whenever I get myself to think about it. But one thing I learnt from this experience is that it's okay. It's okay that you aren't good enough. You can't be the best at every field. And even if you aren't the best at your selected field, it's completely okay. There are always going to be better people at it than you and you don't have to prove your worth. Even to yourself.

So whenever you don't score that perfect grade, tell yourself that you can try again in the next paper. And again in the one after that. There's never a shortage of opportunities. You just have to stop doubting yourself. Mute your biggest opponent. Your inner voice. It'll do wonders for you. Trust me.

As for the time spent studying before the exam, I know it can get tough. Doing 30 chapters in 3 days surviving on 2 hours of sleep with nothing but caffeine at your service. Yes, I can relate.

Exams are stressful.

There is no denying that. The time spent pining over the number of chapters left. Calling your friends to coordinate with them and the constant competition faced owing to the race to complete more chapters first. And then the push you get when you realise that your friend is actually far ahead in comparison to you and you still have a long way to go is unimaginable. All this is healthy because it is prospering your growth. It's Eustress. The 'good stress.

But what about the stress, the pressure, the burden felt when the work gets too much? When the syllabus and time don't comply? In such situations how can one keep going and not have a panic attack midway considering the importance?

I remember crying before my economics final exam paper in 11th grade because of the high amounts of the syllabus, which is inversely related to the less amount of time. Not understanding a single concept of it was just a by-product of the stress.

Of course, the to-do lists and planning helped but at that moment only one thing helped me. Allowing myself to feel the burnout. To let months and months of frustration come all out at once and embrace it. Not holding back. Venting. Ranting.

And that is the last piece of advice for the book. Know that your emotions are valid. I may not know you, where you come from, what subjects you're studying or what time zone you live in, but I can tell you that you're not alone in this. This book is a testimony. Everyone across the world feels these emotions so don't belittle them. There is a stigma about mental health so we weigh our problems and issues with respect to how society would view it. Is it enough to pull it into a conversation? Can it be justified as being 'bad enough to talk about it?

In reality, there's no level of stress, or anxiety you need as a bare minimum for your feelings to be valid enough. Speaking to others, helps you unburden your problems. Use venting as a coping mechanism. You'll feel a lot lighter.

Talking about what you're going through can make other people feel less alone too. You sharing your feelings may help them open up about theirs. Don't ever feel guilty for talking about your feelings. It's a necessity.

If you're going through something right now, I'm sending you a virtual hug. Talk about your feelings. You're not alone. The last thing you want to do right now is to convince yourself that your feelings are real. This is a reminder that your mental health matters. You matter. No matter how invalid it may seem. Use the internet, social media platforms or websites to reach help sites. I promise you'll find support there.

It may be a chronic disorder or it may be an occasional wave of sadness. Know that It's okay not to be okay. What matters is what you do about it and how you deal with it.

You've Reached The Shore !

However long it took, whatever your next step is, what matters is that you made it. You can stop swimming now, you're at the shore. You committed to something and completed it. Take a deep breath and take a moment to appreciate yourself. Smile.

If you can make it to the end of this book, you can surely ace that A. Believe in yourself. Take a moment to introspect your dreams. Your future. You're going to achieve each and every one of them. Sending a virtual hug across your way <3

Kanisha